Note for Parents

Crafts and activities are not intended for children under 5 years of age. As with all hands-on craft projects, the activities presented herein require proper adult supervision. Please note that some of the activities depicted in this book include the use of tools and supplies that if misused or used unattended may present a danger to young children. Prior to allowing a child to perform any of the activities in this book, please make sure activities are appropriate for the child's age level.

The craft projects included in this book originally appeared in FamilyFun magazine. © FamilyFun magazine. All rights reserved.

Craft project steps illustrated by Sharon Lane-Holm

Craft photos by Ed Judice (cinnamon hearts) and Brian Leatart (firecracker hat)

Happy New Year, Pooh! written by Kathleen W. Zoehfeld; *A Special Valentine for Pooh, Pooh and the Storm that Sparkled, A Trick or a Treat?, Pooh's Thanksgiving Feast,* and *Pooh's Birthday Mystery* adapted by Barbara Gaines Winkelman; *Pooh's May Day Surprise* adapted by Cassandra Case

Cover design by Terry Lester

Book design by Niemand Design

Published by Scholastic Inc.,
90 Old Sherman Turnpike, Danbury, Connecticut 06816
by arrangement with Disney Licensed Publishing.

ISBN 0-7172-6413-0

Printed in the U.S.A.

Disney's
Pooh's Treasury of Special Days

Edited by Cassandra Case

SCHOLASTIC INC.

New York Toronto London Auckland Sydney
Mexico City New Delhi Hong Kong Buenos Aires

"Well, you try," said Pooh.

"Tiggers don't do poetry," said Tigger.

"Tiggers can do Tigger poetry," said Pooh.

So Tigger began, "Ahem."

I'll miss April's drippy rains,
*   And May-sy's crazy daisy chains.*

"Did I rhyme it enough?" asked Tigger.

"Yes," said Pooh, "I believe so."

"This is fun," laughed Tigger.

"I'm feeling sadder and sadder," said Piglet. He wiped a tear from his cheek.

"Perhaps you should try another rhyme, Piglet," said Pooh. "There's nothing like a bit of poetry to make you feel better."

I'll miss June (sniff),
When the Wood was green,
And (sniff) all the Julys
That might have been.

"Been what?" asked Tigger

"Well . . . warm and picnicky,"
said Piglet.

"Mmmm," smiled Tigger. They sat quietly for
awhile. Then Pooh brightened.

"I think the rest of the poem has come to me,"
he said.

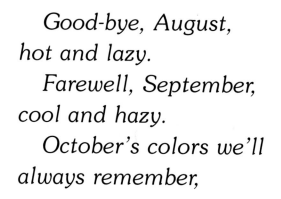

> *Good-bye, August,*
> *hot and lazy.*
> *Farewell, September,*
> *cool and hazy.*
> *October's colors we'll*
> *always remember,*

And the pumpkin pies of
chill November.
To December, farewell,
we'll miss your cheer,
Our favorite month of
all the year!

4

"We don't have to say good-bye to December," said Tigger. "We're stuck here forever."

"Oh, yes," said Pooh. "I forgot."

"F-forever," sighed Piglet.

Toot, toot! Ring-a-ling-ling! Bangety-bang!

Piglet, Pooh, and Tigger heard these strange sounds coming from Rabbit's house.

"Maybe Rabbit's in trouble!" cried Tigger. "Let's go!"

Rabbit's house was filled with balloons and colorful streamers.

Toot, toot! Eeyore was trumpeting on a little horn.

Ring-a-ling-ling! Rabbit was ringing a bell.

Bangety-bang!
Christopher Robin
was drumming
on a pot with a
wooden spoon.

Kanga, Roo, and Eeyore looked on cheerfully.

"I wonder why they're so happy," whispered Piglet. "Don't they know about no more months?"

"Well, it's our bounding duty to tell them," said Tigger. He bounced over to Rabbit's calendar and lifted the December page. "I'm sorry to spoil the festivities," he said, "but we seem to have a big problem. There are no more months in the Hundred-Acre Wood. They're all ended. *Finissimo. Kaput.*"

Piglet wiped another tear.

"Well, I suppose it's to be expected," said Eeyore. "Gaiety, song and dance— it doesn't work for everyone, you know."

"Don't worry, Eeyore," said Christopher Robin, "of course there will be more months."

"There will?" asked Pooh.

Christopher Robin handed Pooh a bell. "Come on! Help us ring in the New Year!" he cried.

"New Year?" asked Pooh. "You mean we have a whole new year ahead of us?"

"Yes," said Christopher Robin.

"With a new January and a new February?" asked Pooh.

"And a whole new March, April, May, June, July, August, September, October, November, and December?" cried Tigger.

"Yes," said Christopher Robin. "And look, I've got new calendars for each one of us."

"Oh, m-my!" said Piglet, "they're beautiful!"

"They're fantabulous!" cried Tigger. "This is so great—we should have a party to celebrate!"

"That's exactly what we're doing," said Rabbit.

He gave Tigger a horn. "There now—no more moping around! We've got to welcome in the New Year with a HAPPY NOISE!"

Piglet smiled quietly. He thought about the picnics and pumpkin pies he'd be sharing with his friends in the new year.

"It's a very friendly thing to say good-bye to the old year and welcome in the new one with your friends," he said.

"Yes," said Pooh, giving Piglet a little hug. "That's just the way it should be."

Tigger and Rabbit's
HAPPY NOISEMAKERS

Rabbit gave Tigger a red paper noisemaker.
"What's this for?" asked Tigger
"To say good-bye to the year that's ending and welcome the new year that's just beginning."
"A whole new bouncety year?" asked Tigger. "Fantabulous!"

WHAT YOU NEED:

- A grown-up
- 2 clear plastic drinking cups
- Tape (colored duct tape works best)
- Any of the following "noisy" ingredients:

    dried beans
    uncooked rice
    popcorn kernels
    buttons
    brightly colored beads
    brightly colored paper clips

WHAT YOU DO:

1. Fill one of the plastic cups with a mixture of "noisy" ingredients until the cup is almost filled to the top.

2. Place the other plastic cup on top of the filled cup so that their rims meet.

3. Tape the two cups together where their rims meet.

4. Once the cups are taped together securely, shake them up and down to welcome the New Year with happy noises!

Other homemade noisemakers:

- Thump wooden spoons against aluminum plates or pots.
- Bang pot lids together.
- Tape waxed paper over one end of an empty paper towel tube; have your grown-up make a slit in the center of the waxed paper; hum or sing into the open end of the tube.

A Special Valentine for Pooh

It was a chilly day in February. Tigger thought it would be fun to go to the bridge and play Pooh Sticks, but the wind was too nippy.

"Well, this is no fun!" pronounced Rabbit.

"Just 'cause we gave up on Pooh Sticks," said Tigger, "doesn't mean we can't find somethin' funner ta do!"

They walked along, not saying much for a while. Suddenly they saw Christopher Robin sitting under a tree.

"Helloo, Christopher Robin!" Pooh called.

But Christopher Robin didn't answer. He didn't even seem to hear. Because no one was sure what to do, they all watched him. But he still didn't turn around.

"That's strange. What is he doing?" asked Rabbit.

"I can't see," said Pooh.

Gopher scrambled up on Eeyore's back. But he still couldn't see what was so interesting to Christopher Robin.

"I think Chrissstopher Robin isss thinking," whistled Gopher.

"What do you think Christopher Robin is thinking about, Rabbit?" Pooh asked.

"How should I know?" replied Rabbit.

Tigger scooped up Piglet, perched him on his head, and tried to bounce high enough so that maybe Piglet could see.

"You're wobbling me, Tigger," squeaked Piglet. "Oh, wait! I can see! He's writing something!"

Just then, Owl landed in the branches above Christopher Robin.

"I was flying over when you all came into

my view," Owl said. "I have halted my progress to investigate. Are you planning a surprise attack upon our good friend?"

"Why no, Owl . . ." Pooh started to say, but Rabbit interrupted.

"Owl! You can help!" Rabbit called. "Can you see what Christopher Robin is writing?"

"Mmmm, ahh," Owl replied. "Let me see . . . 'Happy Vani'—No, no—'Happy Valnite'—No, no—'Happy Valents'—"

"Oh, for heaven's sake, Owl," Rabbit called. "Is it 'Happy Valentine's Day'?"

"That is, in fact, what I was just about to tell you," replied Owl. "Christopher Robin is writing 'Happy Valentine's Day, Wini . . .'" said Owl.

"Winnie . . . the Pooh?" Pooh said hopefully. "That's me!"

"You might expect that to be the case," said Owl. "But you are mistaken. He just finished. He has written, 'Happy Valentine's Day, Winifred' on the card. Now, I must be on my way. Toodle-oo!" And Owl flew away.

"What is a Winifred?" asked Pooh. "Why is Christopher Robin making a card for a Winifred?"

"Because Valentine's Day happens to be tomorrow!" Rabbit answered.

"Hoo-hoo-HOO," Tigger bounced with excitement. "Tiggers love Valentine's Day! Say, what's Valentine's Day, anyway?"

"It'sss all about love," said Gopher.

"Love?" Rabbit sniffed. "Gopher, what are you talking about?"

"A *valentine* isss giving *love* in a card to sssomeone you like," explained Gopher.

"But, what is a *Winifred*?" Pooh said in a sad sort of voice. "Can you tell me why Christopher Robin is making a card for a *Winifred*. Doesn't he love *us* anymore?"

"Oh, n-no!" said Piglet. "What *ever* shall we do?"

"I think we have to give him something very, very special," said Rabbit. "I would give him some of my home-grown carrots, but it's February and they aren't growing now."

"I could give him my best jar of honey," said Pooh, "—the one I've been saving for a very, very special day."

"Yes, wunnerful!" said Tigger. "Let's all go get the honey an' come right back and give it to Christopher Robin right away. There's no time to lose!"

So they all went and got the special jar of honey and marched right back to where Christopher Robin had been sitting.

"Go'n' give him the honey, Pooh!" cried Tigger. "An' then maybe we can find out what this Winifred is, anyways!"

When Christopher Robin saw them all, he proudly held up his valentine for Winifred and asked them what they thought. Pooh was so upset to think that Christopher Robin might not like them anymore, that he couldn't say a word.

"It's bee-yoo-ti-ful!" Tigger blurted out, unhappily.

"Christopher Robin," said Rabbit bravely, "we are wondering—I mean, would you explain the meaning of the word 'Winifred'?"

"Yeah, whatsa Winifred and how come you're sendin' it a Valentine?" Tigger asked.

"Winifred is my new friend at school," Christopher Robin replied. "Her desk is right next to mine."

"D-don't you like us anymore, Christopher Robin?" asked Piglet.

"Of course I like you! Why wouldn't I?" laughed Christopher Robin. He looked at Pooh and asked, "Pooh? What is that you are holding behind your back?"

"Oh, um, this . . ." Pooh fumbled with the pot. "Christopher Robin, this is a pot of very extra-special honey. It is for you from all of us, so you won't stop liking us."

"You silly old bear," said Christopher Robin, fondly. "Thank you for the honey, but what in the world made you think I would ever stop liking you?"

"You are giving your valentine to Winifred," said Pooh.

"Oh, Pooh!" said Christopher Robin. "Just because I am giving a valentine to Winifred doesn't mean I stopped liking you."

"It doesn't?" said Pooh, hopefully.

"Not at all!" Christopher Robin promised them. "Just wait. You'll see!"

And sure enough, the next day, each one of the friends found a special valentine from Christopher Robin.

Piglet got one,

and Tigger found his,

 and Eeyore found one,

and Rabbit received one,

 and so did Gopher.

But Christopher Robin wanted to make especially sure that Pooh would find his, so he took it to him, personally.

"Happy Valentine's Day, Pooh Bear," said Christopher Robin. "Here is your very own special valentine from me."

"Thank you, Christopher Robin," said Pooh. "I have one for you, too!"

Later, after they spent some happy time looking at the valentines they had received, Pooh said, "I think I understand now, Christopher Robin. The more love you give away, the more love you end up getting back!"

"Yes, that is exactly right!" said Christopher Robin. And he gave Pooh a happy hug.

Piglet's CINNAMON SWEET HEARTS

"Instead of valentines, I'm giving all my friends cookies this year," said Piglet. "I call them 'Sweet Hearts!'"

"*Sweet* Hearts?" said Pooh. "Do you mean Honey Hearts?"

"N-no, Pooh," said Piglet. "But cinnamon and sugar are very sweet and yummy, too! You'll like them."

And Pooh did!

WHAT YOU NEED:

- A grown-up
- One large & one medium bowl
- Measuring cups and spoons
- Sieve or sifter
- Large cutting board
- Rolling pin
- Heart-shaped cookie cutter
- Plastic straws
- Darning needle threaded with narrow ribbon

Ingredients:
- 1 cup (2 sticks) butter, softened
- 2/3 cup sugar
- 1/3 cup brown sugar
- 1 egg
- 2 Tbsp. sour cream
- 3 cups sifted flour
- 1 tsp. baking soda
- 1 tsp. cinnamon
- cinnamon and sugar mixture in a shaker

WHAT YOU DO:

1. Combine softened butter with the white and brown sugars. Beat until creamy. Add the egg and sour cream and continue beating until blended.

2. Sift flour, baking soda, and cinnamon together. Gradually add to the butter mixture. Chill the dough for at least two hours.

3. Preheat oven to 375°F. Roll out a section of chilled dough on a floured board to ¹/₈" thickness. Cut hearts using cookie cutter; then use the ends of the plastic straws to cut holes for the ribbon.

4. Dust the cookies with the cinnamon and sugar mixture from shaker. Bake on greased cookie sheet for 8-10 minutes, or until lightly browned. Makes 5 dozen Sweet Hearts.

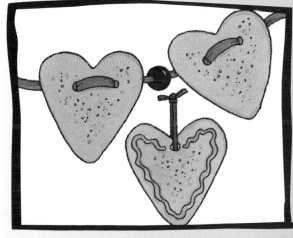

5. When cool, thread the hearts together on ribbon with dried cherries or cranberries to make a garland, or individually, as a valentine. Hearts may be glazed or decorated if you desire. Use your imagination and have fun!

23

Pooh's May Day Surprise

It was the first day of May in the Hundred-Acre Wood. Pooh opened his door and was greeted by sunshine and warm breezes.

"What a beautiful day!" Pooh proclaimed. "This is the perfect weather for a nice, long walk.

April had been very rainy. Pooh and his friends were very tired of listening to the *drip, drip, drip, patter-patter* from one April shower after another. But today, everything looked fresh and green in the sun. Pooh started off happily. He loved this time of year.

As Pooh went deeper into the Wood, everywhere he looked he could see flowers growing. It was so pretty, that before Pooh knew what he was doing, he found that he had begun to make up a little song!

Oh, I love spring
Dum-dee, dum-dum
It makes me sing
Pum-tee, pum-pum
I pick spring flowers
Dum-dee, dum-dum
I could do this for hours!
Pum-tee, pum-pum.

As Pooh sang his song about the spring flowers, he went from patch to patch, picking some flowers here and some flowers there. All those April showers had certainly brought many beautiful May flowers! Pooh was so excited, he hardly knew which flowers to pick next!

First Pooh found some tulips—red, white, and pink. Then he picked some purple hyacinths and some yellow daisies. Pooh gathered little flowers and big flowers. He collected fancy flowers with lots of petals and star-shaped flowers with just a few petals. Some of the flowers smelled very sweet, and others had hardly any scent at all. But all of the flowers were pretty!

Pooh carried his flowers home. He had picked so many, he could hardly fit his paws around them.

When he dumped them on his table, they covered the whole top! Pooh looked at the large pile.

"Hmm. Perhaps I have picked too many," Pooh said to himself. "I don't have enough empty honey pots to hold all these flowers. The question is," Pooh went on, "what shall I do with them now? Think, think, think!"

Suddenly Pooh Bear, the bear of very little brain, had a wonderful idea. He was quite surprised and very happy that such a nice idea decided to pop into his head so quickly.

"Of course!" cried Pooh. "It's May Day! I will surprise all my friends with flower baskets made just for them!" So he got right to work. He pulled out all sorts and shapes of baskets that he had stored away in his cupboard.

"I thought they might come in handy one day," said Pooh as he lifted them out. "And now they have!" He had just enough baskets for all his friends.

Pooh started with a basket for Piglet.

"Now, what shall I give my very dear little friend?" Pooh went to the pile of flowers. "Something small . . . ?" Pooh took all the smallest flowers he had gathered. They were shiny yellow buttercups. Pooh smiled, thinking of the game that he and Piglet liked to play—hold a buttercup under your chin to see if

you like butter . . . if your chin glows yellow, the answer is, *yes!*

Pooh put all the buttercups into the smallest basket, along with some tiny clover leaves. He held up the basket.

"There!" said Pooh, happily. "A very small basket for a very small friend!" He set the basket aside on a shelf.

"Tigger's turn!" announced Pooh, going back to the pile of flowers. Pooh gathered the bounciest, flounciest, pounciest flowers from the pile. He tossed them in the air. They fell down every which way into a flat, nest-shaped basket.

"Tigger will love this!" chuckled Pooh, putting it on the shelf. "It looks just as if he made it himself!"

For Rabbit, Pooh knew he had to make a very organized basket. He chose flowers that were all the same kind—tulips. He made sure they were all

the same color—purple. He carefully cut them all the same length. Then he neatly arranged them in rows.

"A neat-and-tidy basket—just the thing for Rabbit!" Pooh said, admiring his work. Then Rabbit's basket went on the shelf with the others.

Next, Pooh wanted to make a basket for Roo that was as playful as his tiny friend. He rummaged in his cupboard. He found some bright-colored, bouncy balls. He put these in a little round basket with several different colored flowers.

"A fun basket!" laughed Pooh, putting it on the shelf.

Then Pooh made a pretty basket of red tulips for Kanga, a wise basket of paper-whites (with a little, old book) for Owl, and a basket full of clean sticks and purple asters for Eeyore. Pooh hummed as he worked.

Too early for thistles
Hmm-hmm, hmm-hmm,
But asters come faster
Hmm-hmm, hmm-hmm.

Finally, Pooh placed the last and biggest basket on the table. He was ready to make Christopher Robin's basket. He turned and reached for the flowers, but there was a problem. NO MORE FLOWERS!

"Oh, dear! What will I put in Christopher Robin's basket?" cried Pooh. "It's too late to gather more flowers if I want to deliver these baskets on time. Think, think, think."

Pooh looked in his cupboard—no ideas in there. He sat in his chair. No ideas came. He stared out the window. All he saw was that the sun was getting lower in the sky and that it was

getting later in the day. Pooh walked around thinking very hard. Finally he found himself staring into his mirror.

"Ah-ha!" Pooh exclaimed. "I know what!"

He got a wide red ribbon he had saved from Christmas and tied it into a very pretty bow around the big basket. Then Pooh placed in his wagon all the baskets he had decorated and set off into the Hundred-Acre Wood. He left each special basket

he had made at each friend's door. Pooh knocked or rang and then ran away before each friend could see who was leaving their May Day surprise!

But when he came to Christopher Robin's house, Christopher Robin was already outside.

"Hello, Pooh!" he said. "What is that you have there?"

"Oh . . . ! Um . . . hello to you, too, Christopher Robin," said Pooh. "It was supposed to be a surprise. I've surprised everyone. I made them all May Day baskets."

"You are so thoughtful, Pooh," said Christopher Robin, with a smile.

"Well, I wanted to give you something extra-special," said Pooh, holding out the large empty basket with the red bow on it.

"How nice of you, Pooh," said Christopher Robin. But he was puzzled. "What is it? A big empty basket?"

"No," replied Pooh, stepping into the big basket. He sat down. Then Pooh smiled up at Christopher Robin. "This is a Pooh basket. I made it just for you!"

"Oh-ho!" Christopher Robin laughed out loud.

"Dear, silly old bear," he said, giving Pooh a big, happy hug. "You are the best surprise ever!"

Pooh's HOMEMADE POTPOURRI

"Think, think, think," Pooh said to himself. "Flowers bloom for such a short time. I wonder if I might find a way to enjoy their sweetness long after their blossoms have faded?"

Help Pooh enjoy the smells of springtime in any season by combining ingredients from nature in a homemade potpourri.

WHAT YOU NEED:

- A grown-up
- Fresh flowers
- Large bowl
- Natural scented oils
- Fabric swatches cut in squares of at least 8 inches by 8 inches (scarves, handkerchiefs, or bandanas work well)
- Elastic bands
- Ribbon

- Any or all of these natural ingredients:
  cinnamon sticks
  citrus peels
  dried apple slices
  dried rosemary or basil
  eucalyptus leaves
  pinecones
  pine needles
  tree bark

1. Remove petals from flowers and dry them by spreading them out on a flat surface. They should be completely dry in about two weeks.

2. After the petals have dried, place them in a large bowl.

3. Put some or all of the other natural ingredients in the bowl, and mix gently with your hands. Add a tiny amount of the natural oil into the mixture, one drop at a time.

4. Place some of the mixture in the center of a fabric square; then bring all four corners of the square together.

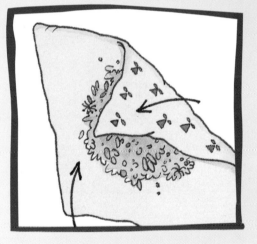

5. Secure with an elastic band, and tie a piece of ribbon around the elastic band as decoration.

6. Give your potpourri sachets away as gifts, or place them in your drawers or closet to keep your clothes smelling like springtime.

Pooh and the Storm that Sparkled

BOOM! BOOM! BOOM-BOOM!

Pooh woke up with a start. "What was that?" he wondered. He thought a light had flashed, then flickered.

"Where is the light coming from?" Pooh said aloud. He listened and looked, but now everything was quiet and dark. Pooh lay down again.

Bam! Bam! Bam! More sounds—but these were a little different from the last sounds. Then Pooh realized someone was knocking at the door.

"Who's there?" he called. There was a little squeal from outside.

Pooh was frightened. He opened the door very

slowly—just a crack. Then he breathed a sigh of relief. There stood Piglet. But, Piglet wasn't just standing. He was shivering and shaking with fright.

"Piglet!" said Pooh. "What are you doing out in the middle of the night?"

"Help me, Pooh! There's a heffalump!" squeaked Piglet.

"Where?" Pooh looked around.

"I don't know," answered Piglet. "But I heard it."

BOOM! BOOM-BOOM! BOOM!

"There! It's the heffalump!" yelped Piglet.

Pooh looked outside. He looked right. He looked left. No heffalump. Then he looked up. Suddenly, the sky lit up with different colors.

"Look!" said Pooh. "A red flash! A white flash! Now blue! Hmmm," Pooh stared at the sky. "Piglet, I believe your heffalump is not a heffalump."

"What could it be, Pooh?" asked Piglet.

"A very bad storm," said Pooh.

"What we hear is thunder and what we see is lightning. The storm is behind the Great Hill, over there." Pooh pointed.

"I have never seen many-colored lightning," said Piglet. "Oh dear! A storm blew Owl's house down once. I hope he's all right."

"We had better make sure," said Pooh. "In fact, we had better warn the others about the storm. Let's take some jars of honey in case our friends don't have any food stored up."

🐝 🐝 🐝 🐝

BOOM! BOOM! BOOM! BOOM!

"What was that?" Owl asked. "It sounded like a seven-gun salute! That reminds me of a wonderful old story . . ."

There came a knock at the door. It was Pooh and Piglet.

"Owl . . ." Pooh began.

"Pooh! Piglet!" interrupted Owl. "So delightful! Do come in! I was just remembering an old story . . ."

"W-w-we haven't t-time for s-stories!" cried Piglet. He was so scared his teeth were chattering.

"A big storm is coming, Owl," announced Pooh. "Here's a pot of honey for you so that you don't have to go out for more food."

"Thank you, Pooh!" said Owl. "This reminds me of my Aunt Sal. She stored up large amounts of food every winter so that no one ran out. I do thank you." Owl bowed gratefully.

"You are very welcome, Owl," Pooh said. "But now we must go warn Rabbit."

🐝 🐝 🐝 🐝

When they arrived at Rabbit's house, they found Rabbit outside looking up at the sky.

"Oh good, you're here," said Rabbit when he saw Pooh, Piglet, and Owl. "Something is

falling from the sky. I do not yet know what it is. But the noise is so loud that there must be *something* falling down."

"What you hear is thunder, Rabbit," said Pooh. "There's a terrible storm behind the Great Hill. Here's a pot of honey, so that you don't have to go out for more food."

"Thank you Pooh," said Rabbit, taking the pot. "But how can there be a storm if there are no clouds? We must organize ourselves to take turns keeping watch."

"W-w-watching for what?" Piglet wanted to know.

"Pooh, you take the next turn," Rabbit went right on. "Piglet, the one after that, and then Owl can take his turn. I've been watching the sky for a long time now, so I've done my turn."

BOOM! BOOM! BOOM! BOOM!

"It's the thunder," said Piglet.

"We've got to warn Tigger," said Pooh.

"Wait! Let's split up. I'll warn Christopher Robin," said Rabbit.

"Pooh and Piglet, you go warn Tigger. Owl, you fly over to warn Kanga and Roo. We will all meet back here at my house."

Pooh and Piglet got to Tigger's house, but Tigger was gone. Owl flew to Kanga and Roo's house, but they weren't there. Rabbit ran to Christopher Robin's house, but he wasn't at home.

They all ran back to Rabbit's house.

"Tigger was not home," said Piglet and Pooh together.

"Kanga and Roo have vacated their premises temporarily," Owl reported.

"Well, Christopher Robin wasn't home either," said Rabbit.

"Wh-where could they all be?" asked Piglet.

"We've been through most of the Hundred-Acre Wood in order to look for everyone," said Rabbit.

"Did anyone look beyond the Great Hill?" asked Pooh.

"No!" everyone cried.

"N-n-not the Great Hill!" cried Piglet. "There are so many trees there! Christopher Robin told me never to be near a tree in a lightning storm!"

"But if they are there, then we must save them!" said Pooh. "Hurry!"

So they all went. They pushed or rode or flew or climbed up the Great Hill.

As they got higher, the BOOMS got louder and louder.

"I w-w-wish Christopher Robin was here," cried Piglet. The lightning was sparkly red, green, gold, and blue. It made pretty, round patterns in the sky.

The friends stopped short at the top of the hill and stared up at the sky.

"What kind of storm *is* this?" asked Pooh. Then they saw Christopher Robin. He was waving to them.

"Happy Fourth of July!" cried Christopher Robin. "Come watch the fireworks!"

"But, Christopher Robin," said Pooh, "we've come to save you from the lightning storm."

"Silly old bear!" said Christopher Robin. "It is not a thunder-and-lightning storm! Those are fireworks to celebrate this special day. Come and watch!"

And that is just what they did.

"Ooooooo," said Pooh.

"Aaahhh," said Piglet.

"Ohhhhh," said Rabbit.

"Wonderful!" said Owl.

Piglet and Pooh's
FANCY FOURTH OF JULY HAT

Christopher Robin told all the friends to bring flags to the Fourth of July parade. But Piglet was afraid he would be too short to wave his flag above the crowd. Then Pooh had an idea, and in no time at all Piglet and Pooh both had flag hats that would stand up high in the crowd.

You can have one too!

WHAT YOU NEED:

- A grown-up
- 2 full sheets of newspaper
- Ruler and pencil
- Red, white, and blue tempera paints
- Scissors
- Wide paintbrush
- White construction paper
- Tape and glue

46

WHAT YOU DO:

1. Unfold both newspaper sheets, one on top of the other, as if you were reading them. Tape the two sheets together and treat them as a single sheet.

2. Measure 3½ inches from the bottom edge of the sheet. Draw a line at that height across the sheet. Fold the bottom edge of the paper up to that line. Now fold again *on* the line and flatten the fold to make the hat band.

3. Paint the hat band blue. After it dries, turn the sheet over. Paint broad red and white stripes on this side of the sheet from top to bottom. (This will be the inside of the hat.)

4. While waiting for the stripes to dry, draw star shapes on the construction paper. Have a grown-up help you cut them out. When all the paint is dry, glue the stars to the hat band.

5. Have your grown-up wrap the hat band around your head. Securely tape the place where it overlaps. At this point, the hat will be a tall cylinder.

6. Take the hat off your head. Your grown-up will help you make long cuts, an inch or so apart, that extend from the top to halfway down the cylinder. These fringes should hang down to the top of the hat band so that the red and white stripes show. Now you can celebrate in style with Piglet and Pooh!

A Trick or a Treat?

"What a beautiful sunset," sighed Pooh.

"Yes, it is a peaceful time of the day," said Rabbit.

"My tummy tells me it is also a time of the day for something sweet to eat!" chuckled Pooh.

"Hoo-hoo-HOO! Well, you're in luck, Pooh Boy!" cried Tigger. "Guess what day it is?"

"Um . . . Tuesday?" asked Pooh.

"Maybe so, and maybe not," Tigger answered. "But it doesn't matter, 'cause whatever it is, it's also Halloween! Time to go out for yummy treats to eat! We better hurry and make our costumes."

"H-h-halloween is h-here already?" asked Piglet.

"Halloween is fun!" said Tigger. "It's a tigger's favorite holiday. It's a time of grrrowly things! Grrrr!"

"I've g-got to get home!" cried Piglet. "I need to g-get ready for H-halloween. I'll put food, a pillow, and a blanket under my bed and h-hide there 'til it's over." With that, Piglet ran away home.

"Oh, bother," said Pooh. "See that, Tigger? You scared Piglet. We have to help him *not* be scared. How can we help him to like Halloween?"

"I know!" said Christopher Robin. "You should all wear costumes that are *not* scary. Then go over to his house and invite him to come trick-or-treating!"

"*All* costumes are scary to Piglet," sniffed Rabbit.

"Christopher Robin, what's the difference between a scary costume and one that is *not* scary?" Pooh wanted to know.

"Well," Christopher Robin explained, "when you put on a scary costume you just want to raise your hands like a monster and say 'Boo!'"

"Sssay, that *is* ssscary!" said Gopher to Eeyore.

"He doesn't even have a costume on!" nodded Eeyore.

"Christopher Robin, let me guess," said Pooh. "A *not*-scary costume is one that when you wear it you *don't* want to raise your arms and say 'Boo!'. . . such as a honeybee, perhaps? If I were a honeybee," Pooh continued, "I would not want to say, 'Boo!' I would want to say, 'Hello, there! Won't you have some delicious honey?'"

51

"Exactly, Pooh Bear!" said Christopher Robin.

"Hoo-hoo-hoo-HOO!" laughed Tigger. "My costume will be fun, not grrrowly. Tiggers always like fun!"

"That sounds great, Tigger!" said Christopher Robin.

"It hasta be a bounce-able costume, though," explained Tigger.

"What *is* a bounce-able costume?" Rabbit asked.

"A bounce-able costume is one that you can bounce in, o'course!" said Tigger, bouncing to show what he meant.

"So it can't be boxy?" asked Pooh.

"Or . . . draggy?" added Eeyore.

"And it must be fun!" finished Christopher Robin.

"Yep!" laughed Tigger. "I love hoo-hoo Halloween!"

"Let's go make our costumes!" Christopher Robin said, and everybody went home to do just that.

Pooh thought and thought. How could he make a honeybee costume? While he was thinking, he had a little snack.

"I get my best ideas while I am eating honey," Pooh said. And sure enough, after his third swallow he jumped to his feet.

"My treasure chest!" he exclaimed. He looked through his treasure chest and found just what he needed. When he was done, he looked in the mirror.

"Hello, Pooh Bee!" said Pooh to his reflection. "I'll bet you'd like some delicious honey!"

Pooh went out into the Hundred-Acre Wood to find the others.

"Hello, Mr. Bee!" said Gopher to Pooh.

Pooh had almost run right into Gopher, because he didn't see him at first.

"Why, hello Mr. . . . Mr. . . . Um, Gopher, what is it you are supposed to be?"

"Why I am . . . I am . . . sssay, I'm not sssure! Jussst an un-ssscary thing!" announced Gopher.

"Yes, I see!" said Pooh. "And you are wearing a wonderful, un-scary-thing costume that looks like a cozy blanket!"

"Thank you, Pooh!" replied Gopher.

"Gotcha!" shouted Tigger-the-Hero, bouncing up and squirting Pooh with some water.

"You've just been zapped with my super-sonic special sauce! Hoo-hoo-hoo-HOO!" Pooh, Gopher, and Tigger laughed and laughed.

"You sssure made a fun cossstume, Tigger!" said Gopher. "And look behind you. Even Eeyore's fun!"

"I hope it's not too scary for little Piglet, though," worried Eeyore.

"Oh, no, Eeyore," said Pooh. "I don't expect so."

"Naw, Donkey Boy!" cried Tigger. "You're a very friendly-lookin' clown!"

Just then Rabbit arrived.

"Oh! You are a cloud," cried Tigger. "An' here comes the rain!" He raised his water shooter.

"Don't you dare squirt *or* bounce me, Tigger!" Rabbit warned. "Besides, I'm supposed to be a sunny-day cloud, not a rainy-day cloud."

"Fantabulous!" cried Tigger.

"Are we going to trick-or-treat Piglet, or what?" Rabbit asked. So they walked to Piglet's house and knocked on the door. No one answered.

"Maybe the little guy went out," suggested Tigger.

"I don't think so, Tigger," Rabbit answered. "Piglet wouldn't go out on Halloween."

"The door looks open, just a little," said Pooh. "Perhaps we should go inside?"

They opened the door and stepped into the house.

WOOSH! Their feet went out from under them.

"Yiiikes!" yelled Tigger. He was scared!

Everyone skidded across Piglet's newly waxed floor and slid right under his bed. It was quiet for a moment. Then they heard

footsteps coming toward the bed. The friends began to shiver with fright.

"TRICK OR TREAT!" shouted Piglet, picking up the edge of his coverlet. He started to laugh.

"Was that YOU?" cried Tigger. "Boy, you had ME scared, Piglet! How didja do that, huh?"

"I waxed up my floors and then I hid behind the door!" giggled Piglet. "I knew you all would come!"

"See, Piglet?" said Pooh. "Halloween is a fun time!"

"That's right!" said Tigger.

"Yes, I think so, too!" said Piglet. "Happy Halloween, everyone!"

"And now," said Pooh, "let's all go trick-or-treat at Christopher Robin's house!" And so they did.

Tigger's EGG CARTON PUMPKINS

As Tigger trick-or-treated with his friends through the Hundred-Acre Wood, he made up a song to keep from being frightened by scary noises:

Oh! When I stop and remember
Ol' Halloween's full of pretends,
Then gobbledy-ghosts
And pumpkins and bats
All become my friends!

WHAT YOU NEED:

- A grown-up
- Cardboard egg carton
- Scissors
- Glue
- Orange acrylic paint
- Paintbrush
- Paper clip
- Green pipe cleaners and/or crepe paper
- Black marker

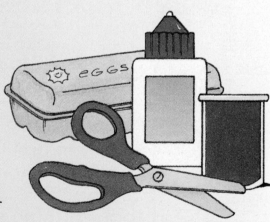

WHAT YOU DO:

1. Have a grown-up cut two individual "cups" from the egg carton.

2. Place a few drops of glue on the top edge of one cup; then turn the second cup upside down and glue it to the first cup, making sure the edges match up.

3. After the glue dries, paint the entire shell with orange paint.

4. When the paint is dry, use the end of the paper clip to poke a hole in the top of the pumpkin. Make a stem and curly vines or leaves out of the green pipe cleaners and crepe paper, pushing the ends through the hole.

5. Use the marker to draw faces or other designs on your pumpkins.

Pooh's Thanksgiving Feast

"I called this meeting because we have a lot of work to do for Thanksgiving," said Rabbit, knocking on Pooh's door.

There was no answer. "The meeting was set for here—now. Where could Pooh possibly be?"

Pooh was up the hill.

"Where is everybody?" wondered Pooh. "Weren't we supposed to have our Thanksgiving feast today?" He glanced down the hill.

"Oh, my! What are they doing down at my house?"

The feast was meant to be on the hill. We're supposed to be eating right now. Helloo!" he called.

"Perhaps I'll just open the honey. They'll be here soon," Pooh said to himself.

"Mmmmm," Pooh smiled. "Just a smackerel while I'm waiting." He dipped a paw into the honey.

Down the hill, Tigger pressed his face up close to Pooh's window.

"He's not in there!" he said. "Nobuddy's home."

Just then, Owl swooped down and joined them.

"I propose we commence the meeting now, Rabbit. When Pooh arrives, we'll provide a full explanation of what has transpired."

"Good idea, Beak Lips," said Tigger. "An' I wanna call this meetin' to order. Ah-hem!" Tigger cleared his throat.

Oh Pooh, dear Pooh,
Now where are you?
Oh Pooh, dear Pooh,
We got lots ta do!
It's Thanksgiving today,
And you are away!

Tigger laughed at his silly little poem.

"This is not a time to be funny, Tigger," said Rabbit, sternly. "The subject is Thanksgiving and what to bring. Kanga, you always cook such delicious things! What would you like to make?"

"I've made a cake," answered Kanga.

"And I helped," added Roo.

"I, of course, will bring carrots," said Rabbit, "fresh from my garden."

"I'll bring thistles," said Eeyore. "No one else would think of it," he mumbled to Roo.

63

"Your turn, Piglet," said Rabbit.

"Haycorn pie," answered Piglet. "But I think we should all look for Pooh, to see where he might be. We don't want him to miss our feast."

Pooh was still up on the hill. He had almost finished the honey. It puzzled him to see that his friends were still down at his house.

"Come on up, everyone!" he called. "I have a feast for you! It's all here. Let's celebrate!"

But Pooh's mouth was full of sticky honey. When he called, no one could hear him. Wondering what to do, Pooh scratched his ear. Then he said, "Oh, bother!" Honey was getting

everywhere. He had forgotten to bring napkins. He would have to go back down the hill to his house, after all.

Just as he stood up, though, he saw Piglet climbing toward him.

"Pooh!" exclaimed Piglet. "There you are! We were looking for you. We were worried when you didn't show up for the meeting at your house."

"Hello, little Piglet!" cried Pooh. "What meeting are you talking about?

"Rabbit called a meeting about what to bring to Thanksgiving," Piglet replied. "The meeting was at your house."

"Oh," said Pooh. "Well, help yourself! The feast is all here."

"What feast, Pooh?" asked Piglet.

"The Thanksgiving feast! I made it for everyone!" said Pooh. "I thought you'd all join me!"

"Join you, Pooh?" asked Rabbit, arriving at the top of the hill. "Why are you up here? You missed the meeting about Thanksgiving."

"I'm up here, because I made a Thanksgiving feast for everyone," answered Pooh. "Won't you join me?"

"Why, how nice, Pooh, dear!" said Kanga, as she and Roo came up the hill with Gopher and Eeyore.

"Yummy!" Roo piped up.

"Sssay, thisss isss ssscrumptious!" whistled Gopher.

"You even thought of thistles!" said Eeyore.

Then Tigger bounced up and hugged Pooh.

"Good job, Pooh Boy!" Tigger announced. "What an incredibibble Thanksgiving feast! And ta think ya made it all by yerself. Let's eat!"

"Ah! My boy!" called Owl. "Your whereabouts had us all in a flap. Fancy everyone convening at this elevated location!"

"This is just wonderful, Pooh!" said Kanga. "Thank you!"

"Thank you, Pooh!" everyone said together.

"You are all welcome!" said Pooh, with a smile.

"Hello, everyone!" It was Christopher Robin.

66

"Hello, Christopher Robin!" everyone shouted.

"Well, Pooh, is your Thanksgiving feast over yet?" asked Christopher Robin.

"How did you know about it?" said Pooh.

"Silly old bear, did you forget?" said Christopher Robin. "You were to have Thanksgiving for everyone in the Hundred-Acre Wood, and I was coming from my grandma's to join you for Thanksgiving dessert."

"Oh, bother, yes," said Pooh. "I remember now. I *am* a bear of very little brain!"

"Ha!" shouted Tigger, "An' talk about forgettin', I forgot to tell you about the meetin' at your house! No wonder you were here by yourself!"

"You are both silly!" laughed Christopher Robin. "Now, are you all ready for Thanksgiving dessert?"

"What's a Thanksgiving dessert, Christopher Robin?" asked Roo.

"It's a dessert that you eat with a 'thank you' in your heart, dear," said Kanga.

"Oh bother!" mumbled Pooh. "I don't have any desserts for thanking in my heart!"

"Well, never mind, dear. I made a cake," said Kanga.

"Kanga!" Rabbit turned around. "That's right! You already made dessert! We can always depend on you! Thank you. And Pooh!—you made this delicious feast with no planning at all! You're a wonderful friend. You all are," said Rabbit.

"Thanks for the thistles," said Eeyore.

"We all are thankful, aren't we, Piglet?" said Gopher.

"Oh, yes indeed!" Piglet replied.

"Hoo-hoo-hoo!" cried Tigger. "Everyone's being thankful! It's a real thank-fest!"

"A Thanksgiving Feast!" corrected Owl.

"A Thanksgiving feast in our hearts!" cried Roo.

Everybody laughed and hugged. Then they all cleaned up from the feast and went back down the hill for their yummy Thanksgiving dessert.

Kanga and Roo's
LEAF PRINT CARDS

"Thanksgiving, thanks giving, thanks giving thanks. . . . *Giving thanks!*" exclaimed Roo.

"That's right, dear," said Kanga. "At Thanksgiving, we *give thanks* for many things, including friends and family."

Smiling, Roo said, "For each friend I am thankful for, I will make a card and fill it with special thanks!"

WHAT YOU NEED:

- A grown-up
- Autumn leaves
- Construction paper (pale colors work best)
- Newspaper
- Poster paints
- Paintbrushes
- Colored pencils

WHat You DO:

1. Go outside. Collect lots of different autumn leaves and bring them home.

2. Spread out newspaper to work on. Place a leaf on top of the newspaper, and cover the front of the leaf with paint using a paintbrush. (Do one leaf at a time!)

3. Fold a piece of construction paper in half. Place the leaf, painted-side down, on the front of the card. Press down on it gently, then remove the leaf. (You may need to try this a few times to decide how much paint works best.)

4. Repeat with other leaves and let dry; then use colored pencils to add holiday greetings on the front and inside of the card.

Leaf Rubbing

To make pretty leaf cards without using paint, try this:

- Use flat, freshly-fallen leaves.

- Take a blank note card or fold a piece of letter paper in half. Place a leaf, underside up, inside the card. Close the card.

- On the front of the card, gently rub back and forth with your colored pencil. You will begin to see the shape of the leaf as you work.

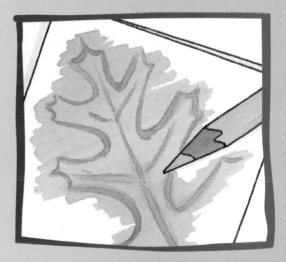

Pooh's Birthday Mystery

Pooh woke up happy. It was such a nice day that he took his morning pot of honey outside and sat down by a big tree to enjoy his breakfast.

"I have the funniest feeling about today," Pooh said to himself. "Something is different about this morning. What could it be? Think, think, think."

Pooh was thinking hard when he saw Piglet and Eeyore coming toward him. They were talking together.

"Piglet! Eeyore! Good morning," Pooh called. "Perhaps you can help. I'm trying to remember— is there something special about today?"

"S-special . . . ?" stammered Piglet. "H-how do you m-mean, Pooh?"

"It feels as if something is supposed to happen today," Pooh explained, "but I can't think what it is."

"Hmm," said Eeyore, looking embarrassed.

"I'm s-sorry, Pooh, but we have to g-go!" Piglet said quickly. His nose turned very pink and his ears twitched. "'Bye, Pooh!" Piglet and Eeyore hurried away.

"Strange!" thought Pooh. "I wonder where they are going? And why didn't they ask me to come, too?"

Pooh noticed Owl passing swiftly overhead.

"Oh, hello, Owl!" called Pooh. "Can you see where Piglet and Eeyore are going?"

"Er, ahh, ahem!" blustered Owl. "I am afraid my view is obfuscated by the foliage just now. Sorry, I must fly!" And away he flew. Pooh walked down the path.

"Why is everyone hurrying this morning?" he sighed. It was puzzling. And he still couldn't think why today felt different, either.

Suddenly he saw Christopher Robin and Kanga talking.

"Christopher Robin! Kanga!" cried Pooh. "Where is everybody going? Is something special happening today?"

Christopher Robin and Kanga stopped talking and looked at each other. Kanga took a deep breath.

"Pooh, dear!" she said. "Now isn't that funny! We were just talking about you and here you are! How are you today, dear?"

"I am fine, thank you, Kanga," said Pooh. "But where is everybody running to today?"

"Running to, dear?" Kanga asked.

"I didn't see anyone running, Pooh," said Christopher Robin. "Did you, Kanga?"

"No," Kanga replied. "Nobody *running* . . ."

"Well, Pooh Bear," said Christopher Robin, "Kanga and I have an important job we have to do right now. May we come see you later, at about three o'clock? Is that all right with you?"

"Three o'clock?" said Pooh, uncertainly. "How long is three o'clock?"

"A little while after lunch, dear," said Kanga, as she left with Christopher Robin.

Now Pooh was even more confused. Nobody could answer his question, and everybody was busy.

"Well, I just had breakfast," he said to himself. "I don't suppose it is lunchtime yet."

Pooh was trying to figure out when three o'clock would be when Rabbit and Tigger appeared suddenly. Tigger made an enormous bounce.

"Hiya, Buddy Boy!" said Tigger. "Happy B . . ."

"GOOD MORNING, POOH!" Rabbit quickly interrupted in a very loud voice. Pooh, you look so tired!"

"I do?" asked Pooh.

"Oh yes, Pooh," answered Rabbit. "You need a nap. I know the perfect place for you to nap! Follow me." Rabbit led Pooh to a place that had especially soft grass. "Here it is, Pooh! Perfect for a nap!"

"I expect you are right, Rabbit," said Pooh. "I had a big breakfast, and this has been a very confusing morning. I am rather sleepy."

"Good, Pooh," Rabbit replied. "Have a nice nap. We'll see you when you wake up. Come along, Tigger."

After Tigger and Rabbit had walked a little way, Rabbit whispered, *"Tigger! You almost ruined the surprise party!"*

"Did someone say 'surprise party'? Hoo-hoo-hoo!" laughed Tigger. "I love surprise parties!"

"Be *quiet*, Tigger!" hissed Rabbit. "Don't let Pooh hear! We're planning a surprise birthday party for Pooh, and you almost gave away the surprise! Now, come along. We are late for the planning meeting with Christopher Robin."

When Rabbit and Tigger joined the meeting, Rabbit told everyone that he had gotten Pooh to take a nap. They were all glad. Now they could get Pooh's party ready without him finding out about it too soon!

"I was just talking with Kanga, and she is making the cake," said Christopher Robin. "What else shall we do?"

"Piglet and I have an idea!" said Eeyore. "We thought we could fill all of Pooh's empty honey pots with new honey!"

"What a wonderful idea!" said Christopher Robin. "It's the perfect birthday present for Pooh!"

"I'll bring food for the party from my garden," said Rabbit.

"Good, Rabbit!" said Christopher Robin. "And, Tigger, when we're ready, you go get Pooh. We'll meet by the big tree at three o'clock this afternoon."

Pooh woke up and yawned. "Naps make me hungry!" he said. "My tummy says it might even be three o'clock!" Pooh was trying to decide which way home was, when Tigger bounced him.

"Hoo-hoo-hoo-HOO!" cried Tigger. "Wakey, wakey, Pooh Boy! Your hour has come!"

"*OOMPH!* Oh, hello, Tigger," said Pooh.

Suddenly Pooh and Tigger heard a noise.

Rat-a-tat-tat-tat! Rat-a-tat-tat-tat!

The sound got louder and louder.

"What's that?" Pooh asked in alarm.

"Don't be scared! It's a parade!" laughed Tigger.

"A parade? What for?" said Pooh.

"Don't you know?" cried Christopher Robin, who was leading the parade with his drum.

Owl made a flying entrance and began to recite:

It's your birthday today!
And we've come to say,

Hooray! Hooray!
We love you, Pooh!
Happy Birthday to you!

"My *birthday*!" cried Pooh. "So *that* is what's different about today!"

Christopher Robin lifted Pooh onto Eeyore's back, and the parade marched to where a big table was set for the party.

"Pooh, we have filled this honey pot especially for you," said Eeyore.

"Yes!" cried Piglet, "and there are lots more at your house, too, all filled up with new honey!"

"Oh, thank you!" cried Pooh. "This is the *best* birthday a bear could wish to have!"

After that, everyone played games and laughed and giggled until it was time for the cake.

Eeyore's YARN WRAPPING PAPER

"I'm not much good at picking out birthday presents," Eeyore said to Owl.

"Well, then," Owl declared, "I'll choose the gifts, if you design the wrapping."

"I probably won't be much good at that either," said Eeyore. "But I'll try."

WHAT YOU NEED:

- A grown-up
- Shelf paper, craft paper, tissue paper, or paper bag
- Scraps of yarn in different colors, shapes, and sizes
- White glue
- Glitter (optional)
- Newspaper

1. Cover your work surface with newspaper. Have a grown-up help you wrap a gift in your choice of paper.

2. Dribble thin lines of glue onto the paper, working on one side of the package at a time. You can draw pictures with the glue or spread it in designs or shapes.

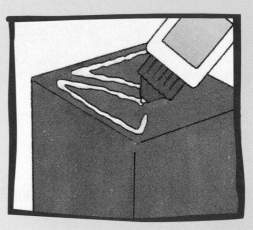

3. Place the scraps of yarn on the lines of glue. Try tying the yarn into bows, weaving it into patterns, or making pom-poms. Glue these decorations onto the package. For extra special fun, sprinkle glitter onto some of the lines of glue.

4. Allow the glue to dry thoroughly. Then, shake off any extra glitter, before giving the gift.

More Wrapping Paper Ideas

The following may also be used to wrap gifts:

- Crepe paper, wound around the package like a mummy
- Bandanas, scarves, or handkerchiefs
- Paper bags decorated with drawings or stickers
- Comics or newsprint
- Sheet music
- Old calendars
- Fancy paper napkins
- Aluminum foil
- Old maps or posters

Christopher Robin's
SPECIAL DAYS SCRAPBOOK

"Do you have a favorite special day, Christopher Robin?" Pooh asked.

"Lots of favorites," Christopher Robin said. "I like to save something from each special day, too."

"Do you save them in a honeypot?" asked Pooh.

"No, I save them in a scrapbook!" Christopher Robin giggled. "Silly old bear!"

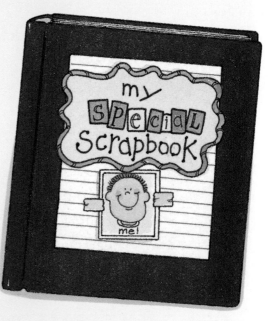

WHAT YOU NEED:

- A grown-up
- A 3-ring notebook with blank pages
- Mementos from special events, places, and people
- White glue or tape

WHAT YOU DO:

1. Group your mementos by theme: birthday things in one pile, schoolwork in another pile, and so on.

2. *Before using glue or tape*, lay out objects on notebook pages so that you can try different designs. Once you are happy with how they look, glue or tape everything in place.

3. Label the pages and objects. (Use names of people, things, events, dates, or anything else you want to remember.)

Ideas of what to include in your scrapbook:

- Photographs of people and places
- List of favorite foods
- Creative writing samples
- Words to your favorite song
- Postcards or letters sent to you
- Self-portrait
- Party invitations
- Awards
- Cards
- Drawings

- Description of your favorite movie
- School memories (favorite subject, teacher's name, report cards)
- Current events newspaper clippings
- Quotations from your favorite books
- Pressed flowers or leaves from your favorite places
- Ticket stubs from events you attended
- Your handprint or footprint in washable tempera paint

85